PULLING

Yourself

TOGETHER

**A Brief Guide to Resolving Inner Conflicts
through Subself Negotiation**

PULLING

Yourself

TOGETHER

**A Brief Guide to Resolving Inner Conflicts
through Subself Negotiation**

ARTHUR S. HOUGH, PH.D.

CompCare® Publishers
2415 Annapolis Lane, Minneapolis, MN 55441

Library of Congress Cataloging-in-Publication Data
Hough, Arthur S., 1928-
      Pulling yourself together: the bare-bones manual of subself
negotiation / Arthur S. Hough.
      p. cm.
      ISBN 0-89638-236-2
      1. Self-talk.   2. Conflict (Psychology).   I. Title.
BF697.5.S47H68   1991
158'.1—dc20   90-21933
                               CIP

Cover and interior design by Lois Stanfield
Originally edited by Betty Gardiner

Inquiries, orders, and catalog requests should be addressed to:
CompCare Publishers
2415 Annapolis Lane
Minneapolis, Minnesota 55441
Call toll free 800/328-3330
(Minnesota residents 612/559-4800)

6   5   4   3   2   1
96   95   94   93   92   91

Contents

Preface

Here is a practical manual for talking to yourself without assistance from guides, teachers, or therapists. Learning and using the skills in these pages will lead you to a recognition of your own subselves, along with all the subtle games they play inside you to get their own way, block one another, and enforce their own needs.

This book can help your subselves become companions rather than competitors, so that you may resolve inner conflicts without the usual confusion or excessive psychic exhaustion. This book will help you resolve your inner struggles for self-dominance, as it examines such factors as will power, rationality, emotionality, creativity, procrastination, desire to change, and resistance to change.

We'll pursue your recognition of the already existing splits within you so that you can invite your subselves into conscious dialogue, reunite the parts within you, and finally experience a whole new unity.

I hope to have included enough of the theory of human subselves to reassure you that subself negotiation is not a game. Your subselves are as true and real in the effects they produce or inhibit as the two hands that turn these pages.

I have been using and refining the two-chair method of subself negotiation in my classes and workshops for eighteen years. I see two-chair subself negotiations work every day in these groups as students become acquainted with their own subselves swiftly, safely, and easily. From often timid and self-conscious beginnings, effective subself negotiation progresses to a comfortable inner partnership and emerges as a powerful, stressless unity. I hope this will be your experience as well.

Arthur S. Hough
San Francisco
January 1991

Acknowledgments

Although this is the first commercial edition of *Pulling Yourself Together,* I have published two previous versions for my students in integrative communication at San Francisco State University. I am indebted to their excellent feedback, and to my friend and roving amanuensis, Betty Gardiner, who edited and published these earlier editions.

CHAPTER ONE

Finding Both of You

When I was a little boy, my mother used to send me to the country for a week every summer to a small farm run by Annie Brothers. Annie was a proper, hardworking woman who took in foster children and raised them. One hot afternoon, playing hide-and-seek with the other children, I hid under the front porch. Annie came out to sit on the porch and peel potatoes, thinking she was alone. While I stayed hidden, I heard her talking to herself. I thought she must be crazy. She was even answering herself: "I don't know what I'm going to do with Billie. He won't behave in school." "Well, I'll just have to pay more attention to him. He needs attention more than the others." "But I don't want to make Carl jealous—he's been here the longest and thinks he has a priority on me."

All these years later, I realize that Annie was practicing folk therapy on herself—very wise, very sensible, very necessary therapy.

My grandmother used to talk herself through her recipes in the kitchen. She and my mother had a standing joke when she got caught at it. Mother would say, "Are you talking to yourself again?" And Grandma would answer, "Well, if I am, I'm not just talking to any damned fool!"

Neither Annie nor my grandmother knew that they were not just talking to themselves—they were talking from one *subself* to another. But it was the most natural therapy in the world, the psychological equivalent of herb tea and hot poultices.

People have always had to work through their inner conflicts, but we live much more high-powered lives today than people did in the days of Annie and my grandmother; we have more choices, more options, more decisions to make. We are freer, but more freedom always means more choices.

Inner conflict, stress, tension, and frustration are recognized disorders of our age. Inner conflict is a painful, confusing, and often a numbing state of mind because most of us don't understand it much better than Annie or my grandmother did. Our society keeps telling us that each of us is a *single self,* which works fine in our relations with other people ("Hello Harry, how are you today?" "Fine thanks, and you?"), but does not hold up when we look at the dialogues that go on inside us all day long, every day.

Internally we are not single selves but plural selves, each of these subselves having a personality of its own. To know this alone gives enormously increased clarity to our inner choices and conflicts. To raise these subselves to the level of clear voices that we can actually hear gives us the awareness to create a final inner harmony.

There is a personal therapy called *subself negotiation* that recognizes this subself plurality and uses it to solve inner conflict to achieve a new sense of harmony, purpose, and self-worth. In moments of conflict, confusion, or indecision, the secret is to realize that you are not one but two (or more). Once you recognize your own plurality, accept it as natural and normal, and make it work for you instead of against you, you will find inner harmony.

TWO CLEAR VOICES

My clock radio is set to play soft music in the morning until I get up and turn it off. On many mornings a conversation starts up inside my head as I wake to the music.

Arthur: It's time to get up.

Junior: Let's wait till we're more awake.

A: But this is the time we agreed to get up.

J: That was last night; I didn't know I'd feel so tired this morning.

A: We've got a lot to do; we have to start writing the "subselves" book today.

J: But it's Sunday; we can write anytime today.

A: Yeah, but you'll want to watch the football game all afternoon.

J: I'm still sleepy; let it wait.

A: Dammit, we're falling behind schedule; we've got to break the ice today and start.

J: Tell you what; let's lie here and think about it; let's list what we have to do.

A: OK. Shower, coffee, get dressed, walk dog, make breakfast, bring in the paper, and clear the desk. It'll take two hours before we can start writing.

J: But it's still dark; I hate getting up in the dark.

A: Come on, don't fade out on me; we're wide awake now. Let's kick off the covers.

J: OK, OK! Let's count to one hundred first. Then I'll be ready.

A: I know that trick. We'll fall asleep counting.

J: No, I promise. Just count to one hundred.

A: Now you've done it! They're playing that dissonant music on the radio. I can't stand that.

J: You're right, neither can I! You win. I'm up.

Arthur and Junior are my own subselves negotiating, as they often do; for me it's an easy kind of conversation. All over the world, people are having this inner fight or another one like it. A surgeon might be lying in bed dreading a tough operation. A supreme court justice might be arguing whose constitutional rights are more important in today's case. A student might be struggling with whether or not to go home for the weekend. A person in pain might be agonizing over whether to call the doctor.

Below are some common inner arguments. Do any of these fit your situation?

I've got to stop smoking.

I'm hungry. Let's see what's in the fridge.

Damn! I shouldn't have told him that. That was dumb of me.

I know there's nothing good on TV, but let's just flip around the dial.

My "waking up" conversation can show us the anatomy of subself negotiation:

1.   Two clear voices: There are two voices speaking, each arguing a point of view, not just a single voice talking to itself.

8

2. Giving names: I give my two subselves names. One is Arthur and the other is Junior. I sometimes call them Ambitious Arthur and Laid-back Arthur. And although I don't like to use broad psychological types, one is clearly the parent type and the other a child type.

3. Using pronouns: I use "I" when a subself is talking about itself, "you" when one subself talks to the other, and "we" when a subself talks about my whole self.

4. Individuality of subselves: Each subself listens to the other and responds fully to what the other says.

5. Rational vs. emotional: One voice (Arthur) is more articulate, verbal, and rational, while the other (Junior) is less rational and more connected to his feelings.

6. Status quo vs. change-agent: One of them is trying to maintain the status quo—staying in bed—and the other is trying to make a change. The subself who has to push hardest is Arthur. All Junior has to do is gently resist. He doesn't have to generate any energy to stay in bed. The key to the argument is energy.

7. No secrets: A curious quality of arguing with yourself is that, unlike opponents in a chess game, the subselves have access to each other's strategies. Since they are both part of the same mind, they have no secrets from each other. When Junior says, "Let's count to one hundred," Arthur knows that Junior is hoping to lull Arthur into falling asleep. The subselves are aware of each other's tricks.

The subselves are not always arguing. Later in my own day, I may hear myself doing *happy talk* instead:

A: Boy, that was a good piece we wrote today.

J: Yeah, I think it was light and funny and made a good point.

A: I think we're on the right track.

J: We could probably finish this little manual in two weeks.

A: Maybe, but we've got to keep at it.

LISTENING FOR THE OTHER VOICE

We all agree on some abstract level that we talk with ourselves as we make plans and decisions, and we evaluate our own worth. We're aware of a swirling, composite inner dialogue. In subself negotiation the trick is to talk to, not just with our subselves. For starters, try this exercise:

1. State a strong intention about some future plan that is not yet entirely settled in your mind, such as "I'm going to go where I want to go next vacation!" or "I've got to confront my boss on this problem."

2. Now make the statement again, and a third time, and wait.

3. Is there a reply coming from anywhere inside you— a voice that says, "Yes, but... ," or "Not me!"

4. Now, make the original statement and then speak the reply out loud as well.

5. Can you give names to the two sources of those statements? This is the beginning of subself dialogue, making the separation between subselves.

10

WHO'S TALKING TO WHOM?

No matter how firmly we believe that we are all singular selves, we can break those single selves down into clear, real, unambiguous subselves. They are plural, multiple, and probably numerous in any one person. We don't have to make them up because subself talk is not role-playing. Identifying our own subselves is a process of awareness. For example, who inside you does these things?

Who makes lists?

Who scolds?

Who raids the icebox at midnight?

Who flips around the TV dial looking for diversion?

Who drinks too much?

Who worries about money?

Who is the impulsive buyer?

Who neglects to write to friends?

Who gets lost in odd jobs when there is important work to do?

Who answers the traffic cop when you are pulled over on the road?

Who says, "I love you"?

Who wants to go to the party?

Who complains at work?

Who wants to work overtime to finish a job?

Who likes to tell jokes?

Who gets sexy?

SUBSELVES, CONFLICT, AND CHOICES

Throughout this book we'll be dealing with three inter-locking concepts: *subselves, conflict,* and *choice.*

When there are no conflicts to be solved or questions to be answered, our subselves are generally harmonious; they melt into one another and we feel whole. But any single individual tends to have many different purposes, aims, needs, and goals. Although these different goals often merge (as in going off to Hong Kong on a business trip and having a good time as well), on many occasions our goals are antagonistic to one another.

For example, a little boy wants to draw on the wall with crayons, but he also wants to avoid being scolded by his mother. Conflict! How does he decide? He lets his subselves take over so he can keep both goals clear in his mind while they negotiate which final behavior he can afford to choose.

In the little boy's example we have the three main elements of subself negotiation: subselves, conflict, and choice. Subselves play against each other, resolve the conflict, and make the choices. When our goals conflict, we find champions for each point of view within us, and as we mature, these champions grow into clear, stable, articulate personalities.

Subselves

Subselves are not just disembodied arguments. They are recognizable personalities that argue for the widely differing goals within us. My laid-back self likes peace and quiet, relaxation, sensory pleasure, jokes and funny things, easy victories, glittering possessions, and being his own boss. My ambitious self wants to be admired, approved, successful, progressive, useful, and important. They are two fully equipped personalities who have known and negotiated with each other for years.

12

Conflict

Subselves are most evident when in *conflict*, but even then we tend to pay attention only to the argument and not to the subself. When conflict arises within us, we go through terrible self-deprecations. When we can't make a clear choice, we feel confused: arguments and counterarguments intermingle with each other like a swarm of bees in our heads. We feel guilty for not being able to choose. We change our minds as each new wave of counterargument sweeps over us. We feel guilty that we can't function. We feel frightened or angry at ourselves when we become paralyzed.

What we don't realize is that we are not merely one self, confused, but a committee of subselves who are not the least confused. Each member usually knows what it wants, and each calls constantly into your innermost ear, "I am you!"

Choices

Our lives are continuous *choices:* As human beings we are enormously free to choose our own thoughts, feelings, and actions, but the catch is that the whole person must take the consequences of each of those subself choices.

What's worse, there is no guarantee that the subselves will always make choices that will resolve the conflicts, or that they will make the *best* choices. When they can't agree, there are stalemates, paralyses, vacillations, mental and physical stress, guilt trips, depressions, angers, anxieties, self-pity, and blaming.

The confusion comes from ignoring the subselves and not allowing them to become articulate voices in the conflict. This is where subself negotiation comes in.

It identifies the subself advocates.

It raises them to actual audible voices.

It locates the conflict.

It forces them to speak their arguments aloud, listen to their opponent subselves, respond to arguments, voice their feelings, and take full responsibility for what they say.

In subself negotiation your subselves are no longer unidentified whispers in the back of your confused mind.

THE PAYOFFS

Here are the practical outcomes of recognizing your subselves and raising their voices in subself negotiation:

1.   Your conflicts become recognized and resolved.

2.   Your stalemates become clear and addressable.

3.   Your cunning and unruly subselves are exposed and invited to a fair fight.

4.   Your personal creativity soars as subselves build upon each other's clear contributions.

5.   Your previously unvoiced goals and needs come to the surface.

6.   You feel harmonious and fully functioning.

7.   Your self-worth improves.

8.   You discover and develop your deeper meanings and goals.

9.   You know yourself in a deeper, more rational sense.

CHAPTER TWO

The Blocked-Action Argument

I'd rather be sailing.
—Bumper sticker

Subself conversation is speaking to yourself, not as you would in a mirror, but from one part of you to another. The subselves can't always be in harmony. The reason that subselves exist is to give voice to divergent goals and purposes within us.

Imagine the similar needs within you clustering together into a subself that takes on a personality of its own. It is quite natural for qualities like responsibility, ambition, rationality, seriousness, and productiveness to group themselves into an alliance to form one subself, while qualities like self-indulgence, pleasure-seeking, and emotionality join to make another subself.

These subselves are our sources for decisions, choices, and actions. We thrive when they function harmoniously, and yet they often don't because they have very divergent needs and purposes. The result is inner conflict. Below our facade of unity, we feel confused, blocked, paralyzed, tense, angry, depressed, exhausted, and indecisive when these subselves are in conflict.

Once you are aware of your subselves, you can easily recognize a conflict between them. The Child subself in us often opposes the Parent subself, the delaying self opposes the action self, the changing self opposes the stable self. Until these apparent polarities are resolved, we spend wasteful quantities of energy in the push and pull of our own subselves. Our sense of self-worth deteriorates, we feel guilty, and we project much of this inner frustration on the world around us and become just that much harder to get along with.

Subself negotiation helps us know ourselves better, but it also serves a very practical purpose. When our subselves reach a stalemate, we can become paralyzed—unable to take action or make a decision. I call this *blocked action.* Here are some examples of blocked action from everyday life:

1. A Parent subself tells us what we should be doing while the Child subself tells us what we want to be doing.

2. The doer subself wants to work while a delayer subself doesn't, which results in procrastination (see pp. 47–54).

3. The healthy subself wants to begin or end a habit, while a resister subself wants to keep things as they are (see pp. 65–67).

Now that you can identify a blocked action, try picking one from your own life and negotiating it between your subselves. Subself negotiation takes place in two chairs placed facing each other. Each chair represents a subself. As you talk back and forth between subselves, you move from one chair to the other. For instance, if you are negotiating a Parent-Child conflict, your Parent subself has one chair and your Child subself has the other. When the Parent stops speaking and the Child begins, you move from the Parent chair to the Child chair. As you negotiate, you speak out loud. Using the chairs and speak-

16

ing out loud makes each subself as verbal and physical as possible. This is not a game and it is not role-playing. The subselves are real entities within you, and they are often just waiting "behind the door" of your consciousness to be heard. You may be surprised at what you hear from your subselves once you give them full voice.

Let's go to work on the most common blocked-action argument: the Parent-Child standoff, or *should* vs. *want*.

STATE THE ISSUE WITH TWO CLEAR SIDES

We can often recognize a blocked-action argument through our use of the words "should" and "want," arranged in any of the following ways:

I should... + but + I want...

I want... + but + I should...

I should... + but + I also should...

I want... + but + I also want...

Don't start with an issue that is already cleanly decided; use one in which there is still some good leverage in either direction.

A short-term blocked action, involving plans for the evening or for a weekend, is the easiest to start with, such as:

- I should do some reading tonight, but what I really want to do is watch television.

- I should clean this place up this weekend, but what I want to do is take a long drive in the country.

17

If your want seems a little stronger than your should, then reverse the sentence and say:

- What I really want to do is avoid a scene with my boss, but I should confront him.

- What I want to do is rest this weekend, but what I should do is devote the weekend to my family.

Or try a long-term goal. Most of us are harboring at least one major blocked action, such as:

- I should save my money, but I want to buy a car.

- I should break off this relationship, but I want to let it last a little longer.

- I should stay in school, but I want to quit and get a job.

- I should step in and moderate this family squabble, but I really want to let it alone.

- I should apply myself to this job and work for a promotion, but I really want to go back to school.

- I should take some evening courses in computers, but I'd rather learn to play the guitar.

And here is the tough fight I find every year in my Alaska workshop students, most of whom get a two-week vacation in the middle of the cold, dark Alaska winter:

- I really want to fly to Maui and lie in the sun for two weeks, but I should visit my parents in St. Paul.

Having clearly stated the issue, you are ready for the starting procedures, which are clear and simple but very necessary. Don't skip any.

NAME THE SUBSELVES

When choosing names for your subselves, avoid using names like Parent and Child, which suggest roles that you think you should play. You don't want to be in danger of *acting* instead of being the subself behind your arguments. So name your subselves from the issue itself.

Saving (my money)	me	vs.	Buying (a car)	me
(Staying in) School	me	vs.	(Getting a) Job	me
Computer (course)	me	vs.	(Learn the) Guitar	me
(Going to) Maui	me	vs.	(Visiting) Parents	me

If you wish, you can use nicknames instead, such as "William" and "Billie," or character traits, such as "Ambitious me" vs. "Fun-loving me." Make sure each subself *accepts* the name you give it. Avoid critical or non-ownable labels like "Stupid me" or "Cruel me."

GET TWO CHAIRS AND PRIVACY

Now, find a place away from people, where you won't be seen, heard, or interrupted, and set up two straight chairs facing each other.

If you like, write the names of your two subselves on pieces of paper or masking tape and attach one to each chair. The signs will help you remember which subself sits in which chair. When subself negotiation gets lively, the chief danger is *chair contamination,* which happens when a subself speaks from the wrong chair.

19

You have now stated the issue clearly, separated and named the subselves, and prepared your two chairs.

START WITH THE BLOCKED SUBSELF

Who starts?

Who sits down where, and who begins? In an issue of blocked action, it's easy to decide. The subself who is feeling most blocked, the one who seems to be hurting the most, is the subself who starts.

How can you tell which subself is blocked and which isn't? Ask yourself: If I weren't going to negotiate at this moment, who would win, at least temporarily? Who seems to be winning? Who is ahead? Sometimes your best clue is that the subself who is winning is the one least likely to want to use the subself negotiation chairs. It is the one who says "This is a silly game. We don't need this." This subself has the most to lose in a confrontation. This subself is not blocked.

What do you say?

The first statement that the blocked subself makes tells the other subself about its frustration: "I'm having a problem. I want to go fishing before the rains start, and you've been holding us to working weekends for a month now. You're pushing me too far."

LISTEN AND RESPOND, DON'T OVERLOAD, ANSWER QUESTIONS

Don't overload

It may take awhile for the frustrated subself to get out all of the arguments and feelings, but don't make this a long speech. The next subself must respond to all arguments, and it is not fair or effective to give a subself too much to answer. Stick to the issue. Stay in the here and now. Don't dredge up the past unless it is pertinent.

From this point on, the subselves argue their points, respond to each other, and try to reach an agreement. This is a very active period. Every time a subself speaks up, you have to switch from one chair to the other, even in the shortest of exchanges.

Arthur: Do you want me to lose this contract?

(Switch chairs.)

Junior: No.

(Switch chairs.)

Arthur: We'll lose money if we don't get on it soon.

(Switch chairs.)

Junior: I know.

Responsibilities of the subselves

Each subself has two main responsibilities.

21

First, a subself must stay in its own chair when speaking. Keeping the subselves separated is the key to successful negotiation.

Second, each must listen to and respond to the other. When one raises a point or asks a question, stop, switch chairs, and let the other answer. Don't ignore arguments or let one subself dominate the negotiations.

KEEP CLEAR SEPARATION: SWITCH CHAIRS FREQUENTLY

When subselves argue inside your head without identifying themselves, the arguments come very fast, often interrupting and tumbling over one another. When the subselves speak aloud in the chairs, the argument should also keep up a good pace.

If one subself makes too long a statement, it is sometimes a signal that something is wrong: Is one trying to hold the floor and shut out the other? Is the listening subself hiding because it doesn't want to answer? These are the best times to switch chairs:

- after one subself has made a single argument or complete statement

- after any question

- after a measurable silence

- when the speaking subself seems confused

- at any point when one subself seems to be speaking for the other one

- at any point when the listener feels a strong urgency to interrupt

Subself negotiations may go very fast or may proceed with agonizing slowness, but the main question of procedure at all times is "Am I in the right chair for what I'm saying?"

WORK FOR SOLUTIONS: SYNCOPATION, COMBINATION, SACRIFICE, OR CLOSENESS TO CORE

When two subselves sit in the chairs and discuss any issue for the first time, there is no guarantee that they will come to an agreement. They are quite busy establishing their identities, their positions, and their feelings about the issue, and they are engrossed in listening and measuring the pain and the power of their partner in the other chair. They may need time to react to all this.

Sudden agreements are not always the best solutions, either. A subself might give in just to get out of the chairs. Subselves often break these quick agreements, which means that we have to bring them back to the chairs again.

There are several very common types of agreements that subselves can and do make:

The syncopation solution

The subselves agree that they can both have what they want, but not at the same time—they agree to alternate. For example, "This weekend we work, and next weekend we go sailing." The conflict lies in who goes first.

The combination solution

The subselves work out a way in which they both win,

23

with a little compromising. "I agree to our going home this weekend for Tom's wedding, and you agree that we'll study for Monday's exam for three hours every afternoon."

The out-and-out sacrifice

Your subselves are not adversaries; they simply want different things to happen at certain moments. One subself issuing orders to the other subself is inviting rebellion and sabotage. But in open negotiation, a subself often will make the same sacrifices voluntarily for the good of the whole person or to relieve the stress of friction. If members of a family can sacrifice for one another, certainly the same camaraderie holds for subselves of the same total self.

The closeness-to-core solution

One subself recognizes the intensity of the other's feelings about the issue, or realizes that the other subself has a goal that is closer to the core of the total individual and that it is in its best interest to give way. "I want my evenings free so that I can go out and meet more people, but I can see that if we go back to school, we'll get something very important that you want (and I'll eventually meet more people there than here)."

GET COMPLETION: SOLUTION, AGREEMENT, STALEMATE, OR POSTPONEMENT

You'll know when you are finished. You have come to either a solution, a stalemate, or a place where you need a time-out from confrontation. Don't just break off and walk away.

Finish negotiating with statements of completion from both subselves:

"Do you feel finished?"

"Yes, this is about as far as I want to go today."

Now you can leave the chairs "together," feeling united again, regardless of how successful or unsuccessful your negotiation has been.

It is important to finish with the kind of civilized satisfaction that will make it easy for both subselves to return to the chairs again soon.

REVIEW

The eight steps of subself negotiation are:

1.   State both sides of the issue clearly.

2.   Name the subselves with issue-specific labels.

3.   Get two chairs and privacy.

4.   Start with the blocked subself; address the one in the other chair.

5.   Listen and respond; don't overload; answer questions when asked.

6.   Keep the subselves separated; switch chairs frequently and with each change of voice.

7.   Work for solutions of syncopation, combination, voluntary sacrifice, or closeness to core.

8.   Get completion, solution, agreement, stalemate, or postponement—but end amicably.

CHAPTER THREE

Dividing the Self: Theory into Practice

We highly value feeling centered and harmoniously integrated. We envy it in others and cherish those moments of grace and effortlessness in ourselves when all of our energy is focused in one direction without drag.

Much of the time, however, we do not feel harmonious. What we seem to need most is inner clarity, and to get it we must first recognize and understand our divisions. We must split cleanly to become whole.

FREUD'S DIVISIONS

Although most of us intuitively regard ourselves as single, whole individuals, Freud saw the self as divided into three subselves: *id, ego,* and *superego.* A Child begins with the id, an undifferentiated mind state in which the individual seeks pleasure. But the Child soon realizes that all of his or her pleasure needs cannot be met directly or immediately. The Child develops an ego to cope with this reality. Later still, from the first ego a second emerges, the superego, or conscience.[1]

The power of Freud's thesis may have reached the professional psychological community persuasively enough, but for the layperson there remained the undeniable sensation of the single I. I am me, singular, one. There is the single I who looks into the mirror, the single I in "I love you," the single I too exhausted to run the last yards of the marathon, the single I who must decide whether to quit the job or stay.

ERIC BERNE'S TRANSACTIONAL ANALYSIS

It took Eric Berne in the mid-1950s to spell out the *multiself* theory in layperson's language and make it at last a part of our common folk knowledge. There are other reasonable multiself classifications, but Berne's division of the self into Parent, Adult, and Child (P-A-C) has become a powerful and available aid to self-knowledge.

Berne's whole theory is based on our consciously acknowledging our ego states, through our experiences as well as through our intellect. He believed that *knowledge of acquaintance* was the best self-knowledge. In other words, it is not enough for the Adult to talk about the Child—the Child must do its own talking. Recognizing the Child or Parent is one thing, but actually feeling it is another.

An individual is not playing a role when he or she is Parent, Adult, or Child. The individual exists in the ego state of one of these three. It is as if each person were three different persons acting as a team and using the same mind and body. Berne

---

1. B. A. Farrell, "Freudian Psychology and Its Implications," interview in Jonathan Miller, *States of Mind* (New York: Pantheon Books, 1983), 235-48.

believed that these states of being are more real to us than the concepts of superego, ego, and id.

FREUD VS. BERNE

Berne's superiority over Freud for self-therapy lies in Berne's three homey ego states: Parent, Adult, and Child. The impression we get from Freud's id, ego, and superego is of deeply buried, faceless forces stoking the furnaces of our psychological lives, but unprepared to stand on the bridge and take command. Berne himself says that "the Child means an organized state of mind which . . . exists, while Freud describes the id as 'a chaos, a cauldron of seething excitement . . . it has no organization and no unified will.' "[2]

My impression of Berne's P-A-C group is of them all sitting around some psychic greenroom, casually dressed, hair combed, drinking coffee, waiting to go on as called, a comfortable ensemble of real-life players.

THE CHILD

Berne considers the Child self in each of us as our first chronological self, the primitive childlike person that we may suppress but never lose. The Child appears to speak for our deepest natural urges, needs, and wants. It is at once playful, curious, loving, spontaneous, creative, open, selfish, cruel, impatient, demanding, cunning, manipulative, and erotic (at the appropriate age).

---

2. Eric Berne, *Transactional Analysis in Psychotherapy* (New York: Ballantine Books, 1961), 48-49.

PULLING YOURSELF TOGETHER

The Child is powerful. It precedes the Parent, for the Child comes first, at birth. The Child creates its own protector, the Parent. The Child is the driving force of the Parent and the Parent's reason to be. Though it is the Child who often appears irresponsible, lazy, and self-serving to the Parent, we should not be drawn into thinking of our Child as the naughty, frivolous, weak, and rebellious side of ourselves. When we criticize our own Child, remember that the speaker is usually the Parent complaining that its needs are not being met. We must see the Child in us as legitimate, not merely as a willful obstructor of our better nature.

THE PARENT

The Parent is our second self, introjected to speak for the survival needs of the individual. Just like real parents, the internalized Parent administers the dos and don'ts, shoulds and shouldn'ts, musts and mustn'ts, and oughts and oughtn'ts. The Parent says, "Here is how we must believe and behave to survive physically and socially in the world. Here are the rules, the moralities, the acceptable patterns." The Parent can be loving and understanding of the Child, or stern and critical (or both), but clearly the Parent believes that it knows how to *be* better than the Child does.

This survival concern of the Parent gives it a special power or priority over the Child, for if we go back to the overall concept of Freud's ego in relation to the id, we know that the ego attempts to gain control "over the demands of the instincts, by deciding whether they shall be allowed to obtain satisfaction by postponing that satisfaction to times and circumstances favorable in the external world or by suppressing their excitations completely."[3] The Parent, then, can be a tyrant over the Child. But the Child also can tyrannize the Parent.

WHY THE CHILD IS HARD TO NAIL DOWN TO CONTRACTS

When your Parent and Child agree on some course of action, you have two wholly different systems trying to work together.

The Parent is a rule giver, thinking ahead, working from enduring principles that say "Do your work, hold your temper, be on time, eat wisely," and so on. The Parent works from a book of shoulds and shouldn'ts, and the book stays pretty much the same. The Parent is also usually given to higher personal morality and ethics, honoring commitment and social contracts—it's written in the Parent's book.

The Child, on the other hand, operates out of a contrary system, putting its energy with its feelings. When the Child feels responsible, it will be. When it feels bad, it acts it out. The Child is working not from long-term goals but in the here and now. What the Child wants, it wants immediately. It is not into delayed gratification. Its sense of morality and ethics ends much closer to personal gratification than does the Parent's.

So what happens when the two of you negotiate a compromise? The compromise will almost always involve a future action: "We will exercise daily. We will spend an hour a day reading. We will clean out the garage this weekend." At the time of negotiation, the Child can be coaxed into agreeing, for in the feeling-oriented, here-and-now Child system, the Child feels good agreeing, wants to get away from the Parent's pres-

---

3. Berne, *Transactional Analysis,* 270.

sure, and is probably not obliged to start the actions of the new contract immediately.

To deal effectively with the Child in you, the Parent needs to take into consideration that the Child will not feel as bound to future contracts as the Parent. Unfortunately, the Parent, thinking it has come to a fine, lasting agreement, may become disillusioned when the Child sabotages their agreement down the line, for the Child's law is to go from feelings, *now*. If the Child is hungry now, that urge is likely to be greater than any previous agreement, valid as it may have been to the Child at some time in the past.

So the Parent must deal with this gap in basic assumptions when making contracts. Here's how:

1. Do not make long-term contracts with the Child. Negotiate a day at a time.

2. Be prepared to go to the chairs frequently, to fortify or adjust the contract. Don't depend on a single, one-time agreement.

3. When a contract is made, start the action immediately, while the Child is still in the cooperative stance, or delay the contract until the last minute.

The Parent does not like to make short-term contracts because it realizes that it can get much bigger long-term concessions out of the Child than it can get when the Child is considering an immediate action. But the Parent must learn to negotiate in the face of the Child's "hot" need, or face frequent breaches of contract, which cause the Parent to lose confidence in the negotiation process.

Use the chairs frequently. Negotiate daily.

THE ADULT

The Adult is the odd one of the three. Where the first two have specific goals to accomplish, the Adult is more a coordinator, administrator, and synthesizer. The Adult stands on three legs, siding partly with the Child, partly with the Parent, and searching the environment for external data, conditions, barriers, and variables that will make the most appropriate final decision in a Child-Parent conflict.

The Adult starts to emerge in the ten-month-old child as the child begins to accumulate information leading to thought. An individual's first two banks of knowledge are the taught concept of life from the Parent subself and the felt concept of life from the Child subself.[4] The Adult subself additionally processes information that is outside of the first two banks of knowledge. The Adult tests, verifies, checks, updates, relates the unknowns to knowns, estimates probabilities, and seeks the appropriate behavior.

The Adult tests the knowledge an individual gains through the Parent and the Child. The Adult, then, stands on three legs of data: Parent, Child, and present environment (the testing ground). The Adult is not an overlord of Parent and Child, but rather a link between them and from them to external reality. In creativity, the Adult often provides the *how to* to the curious Child's *want to.*

Imagine yourself visiting a deserted beach on a hot day, and as you get close to the water your Child subself says, "Let's take off all our clothes and run naked into the water!" Immediately the inner Parent speaks up with "Certainly not! Someone may see us. Someone may steal our clothes. It could be terribly embarrassing." It is the Adult, then, who looks outside

---

4. Thomas Harris, *I'm OK—You're OK* (New York: Avon Paperbacks, 1973), 51.

at the here-and-now situation, sees past the urges of the Child and the rules of the Parent, analyzes the situation, and says, "There's no one around. Let the kid run naked" or "There are some motorcycles up on that cliff. We had better keep our clothes on."

ENERGY: THE KEY TO INNER CONFLICT

You'll notice in the above inner exchange that both the Parent and the Child are capable and ready to mobilize energy and expend it. The Adult seldom relies on superiority of energy, so any conflict of action that might arise among the subselves will most likely be between the Parent and Child. When push comes to shove, the winner usually will be the subself who is able to mobilize the most energy. The Adult, apart from being an influential source of observations and analysis, is not normally a part of this energy competition.

Inner conflict is a natural process of human enculturation, and normal tension is an important part of growth and evolution. For our thinking to end in behavior, we must make a choice, either by compromising or by allowing one subself to secure more of our energy and outpull the other.

On a given Saturday afternoon, suppose that you have a report to type, but it is also wonderful weather to go to the beach. The Child says, "I want to go to the beach!" and begins pulling in that direction with a metaphorical twenty-pound pull. The Parent says, "No, we must type the report!" and mobilizes another twenty-pound pull to oppose the move to the beach.

At this point you are expending a metaphorical forty pounds of energy—an even twenty on each side—and you can't get to either the beach or the typewriter. So far there is no winner, only three losers—Child, Parent, and the total you, who is spending forty pounds of energy to go nowhere. You are creating a twenty-twenty tension and preventing any purposeful action. You might watch television and go to bed early, wondering why you feel so tired—actually having done neither your desire nor your duty.

But suppose the Child in you had been able to generate another twenty pounds of your energy, and with this forty-to-twenty advantage dragged your Parent to the beach. You've made no compromises and no considered choices—the Child simply won the energy war. Keep in mind that with no drag at all, you could have made it to the beach on a mere twenty pounds of energy. Sixty pounds without drag would have sent you to the beach feeling happy and excited. But you are now at the beach using sixty pounds, twenty of it in the drag of the Parent, who is sabotaging your every effort to have fun by guilting the Child with comments like, "The sun is too hot. The sand is getting into my book. We could have finished typing that report by now if we'd done it first. We'll be up all night doing that report." Twenty pounds of sabotage. Given this annoyance factor, it is hard to believe that the Child has really won.

Had it gone the other way and the Parent been powerful enough to mobilize a forty- over twenty-pound superiority, you would have spent the afternoon at the typewriter (or near it) responding to annoying comments from the Child: "I'm thirsty. The plants need watering. I have to go to the bathroom. The music next door is too loud. I can't concentrate. The typewriter needs a new ribbon." Twenty pounds of sabotage from the Child. You either abandon the report or finish it grudgingly. You would have used sixty pounds of energy to do a twenty-pound job, and again no one clearly wins.

Most often these conflicts are between two subselves, no more. The Adult may be a useful consultant, but it is not an energy-grabber. This is why Fritz Perls, founder of gestalt therapy, restricted his conflict resolution chairs to two, not three. The conflicting forces themselves ultimately must come to true negotiation, agreement, and contract, regardless of whether or not the Adult is involved.

Let us contrast the beach/typewriter conflict with a choice in which all subselves integrate their energy. The difference between an integrated and an unintegrated person is clear. As the philosopher Eric Hoffer used to say to his friends, "When you are not doing what you should be doing, you are not able to do anything else either. But when you *are* doing what you should be doing, you are suddenly able to do everything else as well."

When we are doing simultaneously what we want to do and what we should be doing, all energy flows in one direction—there is no drag, no conflict, no polarity. Time dissolves into timelessness, personal energy seems endless, we may even forget to eat or sleep. Such unity belongs to people like the ardent skier who is hired to perform avalanche control at a ski resort, skiing all season for *both* pleasure and profession.

GESTALT THERAPY

In the 1960s, psychiatrist Frederick Perls developed a swift and powerful method of self-analysis called gestalt therapy. His principal device was a two-chair technique. In a variety of ways, including giving voice to dreams, guided fantasies, bodily action, and internal dialogues, Perls exposed psychological oppositions, or splits. He then placed them in direct dialogue with each other, requiring the client to move from chair to chair each time he or she changed subselves. The therapy was quick. Inner doors opened within minutes in many sessions. My own impression when observing this therapy was of an elevator that took the client down to his or her sources of conflict steadily, deliberately, and safely.

At the root of gestalt therapy was Perls's theory that there are two principal subselves: the primitive self and the introjected self. In short, these two subselves resembled the Child and Parent subselves of Eric Berne. It is significant, however, that Perls restricted his theory and his therapy to two subselves, leaving out the more integrative Adult subself.

Psychiatrist Jacob Moreno, however, in his famous subself invention, *psychodrama,* goes to the furthest extreme. When a psychodrama subject goes to work on a problem, every significant input, need, or goal of the subject is given a real chair to sit in. In a workshop situation, other members of the group sit in these chairs and assume the roles of the subject's subselves as the subject has described them. A client eventually ends up sitting in the middle of a cast of twenty or twenty-five characters, each attempting to be a facet of his or her subself makeup. Aside from awesome ego gratification, this technique appears to generate more drama than revelation.

Of all of these prominent therapies, I believe that the one with the most commanding authenticity, simplicity, and directness is gestalt therapy, which is the principal source of two-chair subself negotiation, a method of self-awareness that any normal individual can perform without the aid of a therapist. Yet for underlying and understandable supporting theory, Berne's P-A-C appears to have a clear edge.

CATCH THEM AT IT

Your subselves are talking all day long. But most of us just call it "thinking." Once in a while, however, there is a sudden repartee between two subselves. Try to catch it when it happens. Sudden changes in thought, direction, attitude, or feelings are often the borders that separate ego states. Contradictory thoughts are clear signals that subself switches are taking place in you. When you hear yourself saying or thinking something like this, ask who is talking and who is responding:

A: Well, I'm finished with that. I hope it's good enough.

B: It's as good as we can do, and I don't want to spend any more time on it today.

WHO IS SPEAKING TO WHOM?

A: Darn! I missed the bus.

B: Don't get anxious. Let's just stand here and read the paper until the next one comes along.

WHO IS SPEAKING TO WHOM?

A: I'm going to call the police. That moving van has blocked traffic here all afternoon.

B: Let it go. They've got to make a living.

WHO IS SPEAKING TO WHOM?

A: This is too late at night to be eating all this food.

B: So, we'll skip breakfast in the morning.

WHO IS SPEAKING TO WHOM?

You must have thoughts like these. They are your subselves. Catch them at it, and find out who they represent in you. If it leads to a longer conversation, fine. If not, let it be merely an exercise in identification.

37

CHAPTER FOUR

The Dynamics of Subselves

I'm in love with the girlfriend of my best friend, and I hate myself for it.

—Student log

"The devil made me do it."

—Flip Wilson

We know how diplomats compromise, how capital and labor negotiate, and how husbands and wives confront, but the negotiations between our own subselves involve some departures from normal interpersonal confrontations. The first difficulty not common to other levels of confrontation is the problem of determining, at any given moment, who is talking.

I-MYSELF

There is a folk wisdom that centers around the *I-myself* distinction. We each tend to have at least a traditional semantic recognition that there are two of me, I and myself.

Unfortunately, the *I* often appears in spoken language as the real me, and the *myself* comes through as some anti-me or negative-me. A student of mine voiced this very accurately when in subself negotiation he named one antagonist his "self" and one his "subself," following the theory that the real self is basically good but there is also a little devil subself in us all.

It is common for people to believe that the more verbal subself, the one who most frequently speaks out, is the real self, and that the less verbal, less logical, and often less responsible one is the *sub*self, the weak or flawed voice within all of us. It comes out in our conversations about ourselves:

I can't seem to make *myself* understand this.

I've got to stop letting *myself* eat so much.

I can't seem to stop *myself* from smoking.

I keep telling *myself* I shouldn't do that.

I allotted *myself* an hour a day for meditation.

Before I go to bed, I tell *myself* not to grind my teeth.

I promised *myself* a day off next week.

I push *myself* constantly to lose weight.

I've got to control *myself*.

I've been good to (or hard on) *myself* lately.

I gave him $5.00 despite *myself*.

Every so often, I catch *myself* doing that.

BEAST IN THE JUNGLE

We go so far in this distortion of our subselves that we reduce some subselves to the class of werewolves that prowl around inside us sabotaging our true selves. Note how parentlike the following accusations are as the speaker-self attempts to pass off a noisy, unruly subself as some hidden anti-I force from within:

I've got to break my *habit* of smoking before breakfast.

My *concentration* is always wandering.

My *procrastination* crept up on me this spring.

I often give in to my *need to eat* lavishly.

My *anger* ran away with me.

Weight is a problem with me.

After supper, the *subject* of our sex life came up.

This *feeling* won't go away.

My *disposition* is that I am very unforgiving.

I hope my *slump* has come to an end.

I have a *tendency* to interrupt people when they talk.

I can't help my *feelings.*

I can't give in completely to my *eroticism.*

GETTING I-MYSELF TOGETHER

But there is a positive side to the I-myself usage—it may not be as redundant as it sounds.

When I say "I, myself, never liked him," I might be announcing that I and myself wish at this moment to declare their unity on this matter. My subselves are in harmony. I am the speaker in charge at the moment, but I want you to know that *myself* has been consulted and is in full agreement. This redundancy in the service of reinforcement actually may give power to some statements, such as:

I tried this new product, myself.

Me, I go to every Forty-niners game.

I pride myself on remembering names.

SUPER-YOU POLLUTION

Not all of us are having subself conflicts all of the time. Our subselves have made many previous working contracts as to what lifetime actions and goals we will pursue. But if we believe that in any given conflict there is a true and conscious self, an I, and a subself in opposition, then we ignore an important principle: All subselves are not equally powerful, but they are all equally you.

In his P-A-C theory, Eric Berne insists that one of those three subselves is always the speaker of the moment, not some *super-you* who stands above them all. But the true condition in many of us is that, over a period of time, one subself may gain more power than the other (or others), which results in that subself doing most of the talking and making most of the decisions. This can lead to one subself constantly shutting out the voice of the other, which means that the individual may be very unhappy and know there is something wrong, but can't locate it.

IS THERE A REAL YOU?

Having established that every subself is equally *you* and that there is no one subself who can usurp that title, we come to an interesting exception found in transactional analysis.

The subselves can manipulate each other enough that one subself can possess the whole individual's energy and seem to dominate. We often call this "will power." Subselves have the power to contaminate each other, that is, to move partway into another's territory. Subselves have the power to exclude each other from command functions, and one subself may even go so far as to decommission another. When a single subself is in control of your motor activities, it is called the *executive* subself. In gestalt therapy, Fritz Perls's name for the executive was *top dog,* and he called the excluded subself *bottom dog.*

When you are awake, however, normally you are all present and accounted for. Even though only one subself may be in the executive slot, all subselves are attending, like friends standing around watching one of their number gamble with the group's grubstake. They may be silent (especially when things are going well) or intrude with occasional observations as they feel involved. And, as we know, a subself with a special interest or concern may push the executive aside at any time.

But in extreme cases of neurotic or psychotic behavior, an executive subself can exclude the other so completely that any communication with the suppressed subself would have to be through the executive subself. For example, a Child subself may completely shut out an Adult subself from communicating with the outside world.

And so we come dangerously close to thinking of a subself that frequently holds the executive position as the real self. We seem to perceive one of our subselves as *the real me* if it is consistently able to gather enough energy to pass in and out of the executive position, coming and going at will. You may think of your Adult, for example, as your real self if it has easy access to the executive slot, but during a period of high tension or conflict, the Child or Parent may take over, shoving the Adult out.

SUBSELF BANISHMENT

You are who you are. You have built your subselves from birth, and they are you. You may ignore, suppress, outwit, or override any single subself, but you cannot totally banish any of them. With subselves there is no divorce or abandonment. In moments of angry subself negotiation, I have heard one subself call out in frustration, "Go away and let me alone!" In a normal person this is an absurd and impossible solution. There is no exit for subselves. The imprisoned subself will always be in there, rattling the bars of the cage. To be whole and harmonious is to give all subselves the freedom to be heard.

THE FAST FAST

If you want to meet your subselves in a hurry, just find an issue that will start an instant reaction from them. Consider not answering the telephone for three days, or suggest to "yourself" that you clean house for twenty-four hours without stopping.

My favorite suggestion is to propose to your subselves not to eat for twenty-four hours, but to sit in the subself negotiation chairs each time the issue of hunger or eating comes up. Subselves come to the chairs fully charged and raring to confront at a time like this.

The trick, of course, is not to force the issue with will power but to decide by negotiation. One subself makes the urgent plea to stop eating for whatever reasons it can find and tries to talk the other subself into cooperating rather than merely surrendering, complying, or opposing.

The dialogue goes into new levels at every meal, as you decide not to eat lunch, and then dinner, then snacks, and then breakfast. But you must take all dialogue to the chairs. A twenty-four-hour fast unearths some great promises and compromises.

People who diet are perfect subjects for subself negotiation. One subself wants to eat, the other wants to diet. Any good dieting program should include frequent consultation, dialogue, and updating of the contract several times a day, and certainly before heading into any tempting situation.

AVOID THE P-A-C TRAP

As you begin interacting with subselves that are defending specific issues, you will start to see the larger Parent and Child and (sometimes) Adult subselves coming through. Don't start with them and don't seek them out—let them emerge. To begin a subself negotiation by placing a Parent in one chair and a Child in the other is to invite stereotyping. Your Child and Parent are different from anyone else's, and it is their uniqueness that is you, not their similarity to psychological definitions. Start with issue-specific subselves.

CHILDLIKE IS NOT CHILDISH

Be careful, for example, of treating your Child like a child, an inexperienced and naive adult. Keep in mind that your Child has always been there, inside you, learning about the world with the rest of you, sitting in the classroom, learning the formulas, staying up late to finish projects. It was there when you fell in love and was still there when you fell out. It has seen as much death and pain as all of your other subselves, so don't make the mistake of playing "dear, sweet thing" or "naughty boy/girl" with your Child. It is merely childlike in its attention to immediacy and its priority for responding with deep feelings of wanting and needing. It is the most sophisticated child you know, because it knows everything that the rest of you knows.

In most of us, the Child has reluctantly learned that maturity usually means being responsible and rational, and unless you have made special efforts to keep your Child strong and visible, by this time in your life the Child has had to use every trick it can think of to get out and play.

A good Parent subself knows all this and tries to make compromises that fit the Child's predispositions. Since the Child likes games, many responsible efforts can be cast into a game mode (like the weight chart that needs to be added to every day after you weigh yourself). Since the Child values instant reward, the Parent breaks down large tasks into smaller ones punctuated by reward ("One more chapter and we get to take a long walk"). Since the Child likes activity and movement, the Parent finds tasks that involve doing something active rather than passive and intellectual.

And, most important, the Parent subself tries not to emulate the parent stereotype by setting goals and tasks unilaterally and then asking for the Child's cooperation. The wise Parent comes to the chairs with the Child to help set goals rather than merely to ask the Child to abide by them.

PARENT AS EXECUTIVE

In our current society, the majority of our day's activities have to do with work, commitments, obligations, tasks, chores, appointments, duties, assignments, and schedules. Whether we like it or not, we lead relatively responsible lives. We are survival oriented, and our principal survival subself is the Parent. It is not uncommon, then, for most of us to speak out of habit from our Parent subself. The natural tendency, since the Parent is our main spokesperson, is to think of the Parent as the executive self, the respectable self, the goal-oriented self. With all of this power, it is not surprising that the Parent becomes more verbal, more rational, more persuasive, and more "correct." This does not mean that the Child lacks power; we simply deny it the opportunity to speak. It becomes easy for us, speaking from our Parent, to think of the Child (and even to describe this subself to others) as our irresponsible and incorrect self, to be excused for its occasional bursts of impulsive naughtiness. And remember that when we talk to others, it is most often about the business of life—and it is usually a Parent-to-Parent dialogue.

Our subselves lose their equality when we cast one subself as illegitimate. An early exercise for each of us should be a test of our personal awareness, asking as often as we can, "Who is speaking now? Who in me is agreeing? Who is disagreeing?" When we come to actual subself negotiation, we will have had some practice at sorting out the subselves.

CHAPTER FIVE

Procrastination: The Now-or-Later Argument

*I read the subself negotiations process again and then I
did it. I know that I procrastinate because my subselves
are always fighting for recognition and that they are both
unhappy and that rather than to give leeway to one of
them I do nothing. I know that I will drop procrastination
the moment I start listening to my subselves and be fair.*

(Next day)

*Actually, it was that simple. I listened to my subselves, dealt
with the issues and I have got more work done than in
many months.*

—Student log

In the Parent/Child standoff (pages 33–35) we had two
straightforward sides to the conflict: *should* vs. *want*.
Now we come to a second kind of blocked-action argument: procrastination. We make a cunning omission when
we talk about our terrible tendency to procrastinate. What we
usually call procrastination is only the second act of the play,
the reaction to delay. We completely ignore the first act: the
cause of the delay.

Procrastination means "to put off, postpone, or defer taking some action." Our delays range from work tasks to cleaning the house to sending Christmas cards. Our silent assumption is that we have already firmly decided to perform the task.

This turns the issue into a now-or-later argument, a *doer* vs. *delayer* subself fight. The doer subself says, "We must do this, you know," and the delayer subself says, "Of course, but let's wait a bit." The result is a conflict between the subselves, without confrontation. We then support our own procrastination with three hidden ploys: nonconsultation, the bad-self excuse, and the delayer evasion.

NONCONSULTATION

If we think back far enough, we find that most procrastinated tasks are subself inflicted. Procrastination often starts when one ambitious or responsible subself (the doer) makes a unilateral decision to take some "necessary" action. Only then does the doer come to the previously excluded subself to say "What's the matter with you? Why aren't you helping me do this now? Why can't you go to the library and do this research as I want you to? It must be done!"

What we have omitted is any preconsultation with the opposing subself at the time we made the original commitment. Students whose delayer subself puts off writing term papers often can trace the conflict back to never having previously negotiated whether to go to college and take the course in the first place. The delayer subself may well be the self that would never have made any heavy commitments except after intense subself negotiation and compromise. So the delayer drags its feet to make its point to the doer subself, without actually confronting the doer. We only consult the delayer subself once we have made the commitment and begin to procrastinate.

THE BAD-SELF EXCUSE

The doer subself now becomes self-righteous and tells everyone that it really wants to, and has to, do this task, but that, unfortunately, it has a procrastination problem. Next comes the *bad-self excuse:* that buried deep inside is a stubborn, malicious, destructive, and uncontrollable subself that won't cooperate, as though we are hiding a werewolf inside. This allows the doer subself to save face by saying, "It's not me. It's the other one who won't get moving," an attitude that does not lead to improved cooperation from the delayer subself. The problem is that the doer subself believes it is the *real self,* and therefore depicts the delayer as a mere *sub*self. For example: "Tonight I argued with my subself about making those reservations early. I really gave myself a good talking to."

THE DELAYER EVASION

How does the delayer feel about all of this? The doer made a decision without consulting the delayer. The delayer probably opposes the original decision and most certainly resents being excluded. Now the doer says that the delayer will be responsible for the dire consequences if it does not cooperate. The delayer recognizes that the doer is directing a powerful energy and will cast guilt upon the delayer if it refuses to help. But the delayer is not eager to enter into negotiations on a task that it never agreed to, so it adopts the cunning evasion of agreeing that the job must be done and thereby avoids direct confrontation on the *fait accompli* actions of the doer. The delayer says, "OK, it has to be done, but not now." The delayer can get its message of reluctance across at this stage without engaging in the costly compromise of negotiation. All the delayer has to do is apply the brakes, using its own energy to drag against that of the doer.

THE WAY OUT: SETTING GOALS TOGETHER

The solution to this self-inflicted procrastination is to recognize the stalemate as a symptom that you have seriously neglected subself negotiation and it's time you attempt to catch up. The doer subself does not approach the delayer as though it were a social disease and a malingerer; it goes back to stage one and discusses the original decision: "Let's talk about whether we want to be here in school at all and whether we have taken on too much work." The delayer, then, for the first time, can speak as an equal about its own needs and wants and how important they are to the total individual. Now, the delayer may compromise—but it expects that the doer subself will compromise also—not just on schedules, but on purposes and commitments as well. Each instance of procrastination should signal you to root out the cause, not merely whip a reluctant subself into action.

Procrastination, then, is not the root problem but the symptom of an unnegotiated power play, as when management increases production quotas without consulting workers and later finds the workers responding not with strikes but with slowdowns and sick days.

DOER/DELAYER COLLUSION

It is hard for the doer in each of us to change its strategy. The doer already is convinced of the necessity to perform some task and realizes that to come to the negotiating chairs at this point may mean a compromise that spoils its hidden resistance.

The doer, then, seems to collude with the delayer in being reluctant to come forward and confront openly. If the doer ever really sits down and listens to the delayer, it will have to recognize an authentic (not a subordinate) subself who, in fact, does not share the goals of school, success, money, and status. The doer, then, would rather keep its original list of goals intact, and tolerate the procrastination tug-of-war, and the delayer would rather put off the task than be driven into a costly truce.

Both subselves win and lose at this strategy. The delayer succeeds in making its point without actually saying it, and the doer finally succeeds in frightening the delayer into action, with eleventh-hour comments like, "This term paper is due tomorrow. If we don't write it tonight, we flunk the course. Do I finally get your cooperation or don't I?" When the doer has established a sufficient crisis, the subselves band together in a heroic deadline rush and complete the task. But every so often, they don't complete the task, and you flunk the course or suffer some similar embarrassment.

Win or lose, look at the cost in anxiety, tension, guilt, and wasted time. Remember Hoffer's comment that "When you are not doing what you should be doing, you are not able to do anything else either."

So, in two-chair subself negotiation, we are dealing only with a symptom when we attack procrastination. It is better to focus on the cause of the delayer subself's opposition.

Most often, procrastination is caused by a parent-type subself making unilateral decisions and inflicting them on the Child ("We must write Mother this week"). Occasionally, it is the Child who commits without consulting the Parent ("I've got to have a day off from this grind"). There is even a Parent vs. Parent procrastination when one says, "We must do this," and the other answers, "We are in trouble if we do."

In using the subself chairs, we employ the same structure as in the should-vs.-want confrontation. The doer makes the opening statement: "We'll lose the whole ball game if we don't get this done." The delayer responds with something like, "I really don't want to do this, but I know you committed us to it, and I want to open up the whole issue of how we got to this point."

The secret is to confront *early* and to give the reluctant subself its full, legitimate voice in the original contract. Trapping our reluctant subself is cunning, but not wise.

BUT YOU'VE GOT TO USE THE CHAIRS

My students and workshop clients listen carefully as I teach them subself negotiation, and they go faithfully through classroom exercises with me. They easily can admit that they have lots of conflicts and dilemmas in which subself negotiation would be useful, but eventually they rebel on one point: "Do we have to use the chairs? Can't we do this in our heads?"

The answer, with all the vehemence I can muster, is, "YOU MUST USE THE CHAIRS!"

You *have* been doing it in your head up to now, and still you have conflicts and internal dilemmas. The chairs are not a gimmick—they are essential. They raise the psychological to the physical, the partial to the total, the voiceless to the voiced, the contaminated mess of thoughts invading and evading each other to subselves having to stand up on their hind legs and really talk to each other clearly in sound and sentence.

Vocalizing your subselves puts vague, ambiguous thoughts and feelings into solid vehicles—words, sentences, subjects, verbs, and objects. Speaking aloud throws thought into new dimensions: You must hear it! Speaking is processed by different mental equipment than silent thinking. Silent thought is often too fast, incomplete, overridden, abandoned, interrupted, and disowned. It is just a thought passing through, not owned by any part of you.

The chairs themselves add still another dimension to speaking aloud. They provide a physical *wedge* between the subselves, giving each an entire island on which it is sovereign and cleanly separated from any other subself by the little chasm between the chairs.

Most people complain that there is no place in their daily lives where they have enough privacy to set up two chairs and act out a subself dialogue, out of sight and sound of other people. That, in itself, is a cultural statement of great significance: Not only are we never alone, but we can't easily find a place to be alone. There are, of course, bedrooms and bathrooms and garages and cellars and attics and garden sheds and walks in the woods. Any two boxes in the garage are good enough for a subself conversation. For apartment dwellers, there is shutting the bathroom door and setting up a dialogue, using the laundry hamper and the toilet seat. People put locks on their diaries, and those who are interested in meditation often set up little corners reserved for meditation amid the architecture of their lives. Subself negotiation should have at least this much legitimacy and accommodation in terms of an individual's control over his or her own space.

My only concession is this: If you have problems that you can settle by thinking them through in your head, then do it. When you come to the ones that you can't sort out internally, then get into the chairs and talk.

WHY WE DON'T USE THE CHAIRS

Do we really love solutions as much as we love problems? Our problems so often seem part of our whole complex makeup. Each problem is rooted in our past, our subconscious, our most precious subselves. Long-term problems, like being overweight, drinking too much, needing exercise, tolerating a bad marriage, and so on, become like the cracks in the walls of our houses: We complain about them and tolerate them until some dramatic moment when we are forced to repair them. It seems so inhospitable to purge them with any solution so swift as using subself negotiation.

Why, then, don't we use the chairs? Because sometimes we don't want to solve the problem. We prefer the sitcom solution, which is to endure until the problem goes away, using the rationale that if we can hang in there long enough, events will occur that wash away or dissolve the problem, or some external force will come along to force a solution. We might win the lottery; someone might buy the house; the boss might die.

I urge you to sit in the chairs no matter how silly you think you'll feel or how sure you are that you can do all of this in your head. So, risking your continued irritation with my insistence, I'm going to end every page with the number-one rule of subself negotiation:

YOU MUST USE THE CHAIRS!

CHAPTER SIX

Overcoming the Tricks of the Subselves

F or most of us, sitting in two chairs and talking to ourselves is a new and somewhat disconcerting process. It is also new and risky for our subselves. We are inviting them to conduct their business out in the open, and many of their tricks of concealment are suddenly unavailable to them. Our subselves are like Siamese twins, and we need to anticipate some of the more common problems in separating them.

AVOIDING CHAIR CONTAMINATION

Subselves love to interrupt each other and confuse the issue. In order to keep the right subself in the right chair, we must pay close attention to which one is speaking at any moment. Here are some suggestions:

Keep moving

If you stay too long in one chair, the other subself will become impatient and cross over, contaminating the subself

55

who is speaking. Don't let any comment go on so long as to invite interruption.

Keep your pronouns straight

When one subself is speaking from its own point of view, it will use the pronouns "I" and "me." ("I simply don't want to go to the opera. It bores me.")

By the same token, when it is referring to the other subself, it will say "you." ("You've been a little hard on me lately.")

The tricky part comes in separating the "I" and "you" from the "we" and "our." Use "we/our" only to refer to the total person. ("When *we* go to the opera, *you* always want to stand around in the lobby to be seen.")

It is helpful to think of two subselves as a couple. Each subself speaks for itself but refers to the subselves together as "we."

The confusion comes in saying "I" when you mean "we." "I got a lot of work done last week" should really be "*We* got a lot of work done last week." This all makes perfect sense, even though the possessive pronoun "our" sometimes sounds a little strained. It is correct to say "our" mother, father, brother, sister, dog, and Volkswagen, but it takes a little extra attention to say "our husband" or "our wife" without feeling vaguely polygamous.

Try chair hopping

A good way to keep the separation clean and to keep one subself from sneaking over into the other's chair is to allow each subself to make its own comments and avoid stating or restating the other subself's points. After all, the other subself is right there in front of you and should make its own arguments. Don't say, "You believe that if we go off on this weekend trip, we won't get any work done." The danger is that you may easily fall into making the other subself's points for it, and that subself will then find it easy to slide over and start talking for itself, in the wrong chair.

Clear separation needs special attention when a compromise is being made, so that one subself is not putting words into the mouth of the other. In an argument between two subselves, one of whom wants to buy three new suits while the other wants to save money, who is it who says, "Well, maybe we could buy just one suit instead of three," the *buyer* or the *saver?* Let each subself make its own points and compromises.

Do not use a third chair

In therapy, with professional guidance, a third chair occasionally works effectively if the therapist sees the need to add the Adult to a Parent/Child argument, or a second Parent when the Parent subself seems to be split. But it is my experience that three chairs add enough complication to require a therapist to act as traffic control.

When the going gets rough in a subself confrontation, you may be tempted to put the soothing voice of an arbiter in a third chair. The danger is that this can lead to an easy compromise that avoids direct, one-to-one negotiation. The arbiter tries to make the compromise for the conflicting subselves, and the subselves tend to feel less committed to a solution urged upon them than one hammered out between them. Vital energy seeps out of the encounter with the introduction of a third chair.

In any given conflict there certainly may be more than two differing points of view, and you may have any number of subselves clamoring to get into the argument. In that case, take them on one at a time so that you continue to use only two chairs. Using a third chair opens the floodgate to a whole roomful of subselves, adding, in my opinion, more confusion than clarity.

After you have used the two-chair technique extensively and effectively, and after you have learned to keep up a good separation and strong awareness of who is who, you may try using a third chair for complicated issues. But don't try to take on too much too soon, or you may blunt your purpose of genuine conflict resolution.

Getting the right subselves

We already have established that the easiest method of resolving subself conflict is to name the subselves according to the sides of the issue they are representing (Impulsive me vs. Careful me). We also have suggested that under these issue-specific subselves there are likely to be major subselves coming through, such as transactional analysis's Parent, Adult, and Child. But there are many other combinations available, even from these three. Let's take a look at all of the subselves you might be, just within the P-A-C definition.

You may well have two Parent selves instead of one. After all, most of us had two original parents whose input created our own Parent subselves. There is often the nurturing Parent and the evaluating Parent. One tends to be accepting and the other critical.

Your Child also may split into two subselves: the good, socialized, adapted Child and the natural Child. One is more the cooperative performer while the other is more independent and demanding.

Even the Adult can act at times as a conciliator and at other times as a central organizing self. One takes a more passive role, the other a more active role.

In transactional analysis, the Parent is not a terribly creative subself. It relies mainly on old tapes of what Father or Mother used to say or would have said on this present occasion. Your best creative-thinking team is apparently the Adult-Child combination.

But the Parent is enormously rich in makeup. First, you must consider that you taped at least two, if not several, significant parent voices when you were young: Mother, Father, grandparents, older siblings, other household authorities, and even influential television characters.

The danger of sitting down in the chairs and trying to adopt one of the subselves from transactional analysis is that they represent categories that are likely to be too broad, too narrow, or too stereotyped for the issue at hand. You then tend to act out what you expect this subself to stand for rather than what the subself actually is saying. Subself negotiation is not role *playing,* it is role *revealing.* Stay with the specifics of the issue.

STATUS QUO VS. ONE-TIME CHANGE

Be prepared for a curious division in subself negotiation. One subself may uphold the status quo (staying, saving, holding, keeping, delaying) and say, "Let's just leave things the way they are," while the other may be advocating a *one-time change.* This can be an unbalanced situation, because in a standoff between the subselves, all the status quo subself has to do is hold firm—it is the change-agent subself who must mobilize enough energy to generate a change. It would seem, then, that the status quo subself has the advantage. For example:

- whether to *save your money* or buy a car
- whether to *stay home* or go skiing
- whether to confront the boss or *let sleeping dogs lie*
- whether to start an exercise program or *not*
- whether to get married or *stay single*
- whether to quit your job or *stay*
- whether to *stay home and study* or go out for a beer
- whether to *sit on this information* or tell somebody

The change-agent subself, being fully aware of its "sit-tight" disadvantage, develops a catlike cunning in waiting for the right moment to pounce. All it has to do is generate enough energy to take the action it advocates just *once,* and it has won.

The conservative subself, who wants to save money, has to guard the bank account day in and day out, while the subself who wants to buy a car only has to overcome the save-our-money force once. From the moment you buy the car, both subselves are committed.

Like a thief in the henhouse, the change-agent subself waits for a weak moment. The dieting subself may refrain from eating all day long, but the eating subself knows that at 10:30 at night, discipline is weak and natural urges are strong.

It is this *blitzkrieg* ploy of the change-agent subself that makes subself negotiation so necessary. If the subselves agreed that they will take no new action whatsoever before consulting each other in the subself chairs, the manipulating subself must trade in its trickery for open and rational negotiation.

THE RATIONAL VS. THE EMOTIONAL

Another inequality between subself personalities that we must remember is the rational/emotional balance. In a given conflict, one subself might be the rational, logical, articulate, and persuasive subself (often backed by the Parent). The opposing subself, on the other hand, might be at a distinct disadvantage because the basis for its point of view rests in its strong feelings, emotions, urges, and needs. The Child might be backing this subself. The strength of this subself lies in the intensity of its feelings. The weakness of the emotional subself is that it can't express its argument as skillfully in open discussion as the articulate opponent can. Your Child spoke in feelings before it spoke in words. In many cases, its feelings *are* its words and its reasons. Feelings have a language of their own.

In open discourse, the person with the good arguments normally is expected to win. But if the emotional subself feels overwhelmed by the other's rationality and believes that its own feelings are being undervalued, it can turn stubborn, block any solution, or sabotage a final agreement in which it has felt manipulated. Let's watch these two at work:

Rational: It's obvious that telling Agnes that Bill is cheating on her is the right thing to do.

Emotional: I know, but I don't like it.

Rational: I can understand that, but we can't just stand by and let their marriage go down the drain.

Emotional: Yeah, but I feel creepy doing this.

Rational: Come on now, you know it's the right thing.

Emotional: Can't we just drop it for now? It hurts just to think about it.

YOU MUST USE THE CHAIRS

Rational: Can you think of one good reason for us to sit on this information?

Emotional: (Stubborn silence.)

The point is that both subselves are you. The feeling side of you is as legitimate as the rational and responsible side.

Rational bullying doesn't work, and the rational side cannot always make the emotional side stick to purely rational arguments. Don't get caught in the trap of "Whoever has the better argument wins." Remember: Your goal is harmony.

CHAPTER SEVEN

Habit Making and Breaking: Will Power vs. the Slob

The third kind of blocked-action argument is the making or breaking of personal habits. Once again we are dealing with an I-should vs. I-want issue, reinforced by the old procrastination problem of now or later. What habit making and breaking adds to these two subself negotiations is the need to sustain a personal decision over the long term.

As with procrastination, both involved subselves need to negotiate the original terms of the project. It is no good to fall back on the New Year's resolution enthusiasm, in which one subself sets the task and tries to force, cajole, or trick the other into complying. If there is a subself who wants to start a new habit, there is certainly a subself who wants to keep enjoying the old life.

OLD WAYS VS. NEW WAYS

The subself who wants to break a habit, or start a new one, usually is backed by your Parent. Either you're doing something your Parent thinks you should stop, or you're not doing something your Parent thinks you should start. The common struggles are with:

Habits to Stop	Habits to Start
Smoking	Dieting
Alcohol	Daily exercise
Drugs	Daily meditation
Excessive TV	Daily time with your family
Too much coffee	Practicing an instrument
Biting your nails	Saving your money

In starting or stopping a habit, you've usually got three main conflict characteristics at work.

1. Status quo vs. change

Your status quo subself is willing to let things stay as they are. Your change-agent subself has the burden of convincing the other subself and mobilizing the energy to carry off a new venture. It appears to take as much energy to stop old habits as to start new ones.

2. Rational vs. emotional

The more rational self is saying, "Let's do what's good for us," and the emotionally based subself is saying, "Let's do what's comfortable." The articulate and rational subself usually initiates the argument. The comfort-loving side of you is heavily based on feelings and is not too logical and responsible. Remember to respect intensity as well as intellect.

YOU MUST USE THE CHAIRS

3. Instant vs. delayed gratification

The Parent is always trying to get good habits going and break old bad ones. The Parent loves responsible habits because they are orderly and predictable and involve long-range planning. The Child does not like habits for just those reasons. The Child is spontaneous and lives mainly in the here and now, craving instant gratification and tending to ignore future consequences.

However, the Child can develop a habit strategy out of sheer desperation when the habits of the Parent become intolerable. For example:

- I want us to refuse phone calls and household chores for two hours every night after dinner.

- I want a regular bowling night every week.

- I want to put 10 percent of our income away every week for doing fun things.

The biggest error we make in trying to start or stop habits is substituting will power for two-chair negotiation.

THE WILL POWER FALLACY

Will power is not, as we so often seem to think, a powerful, focused concentration of all of the subselves on some task or discipline. Instead, will power is most frequently a hostile takeover of the individual by one temporarily powerful subself. It is a power grab, and its only purpose is to smother opposing subselves with energy mobilized through fear, guilt, anger, or some other psychic energy source. Will power is not usually based on open subself negotiation.

65

In the absence of an understanding of our true subself makeup, most of us turn to the New Year's resolution type of will power, in which the dominant subself unilaterally lays down the law to the resister subself with no attempt to negotiate and compromise.

The dominant subself (the Parent, in this case) issues decrees: We will lose weight. We will exercise daily. We will stop smoking. We will quit using drugs. We will apply ourselves more to our work.

This failure to negotiate at the outset brings on one of two results. If the will power decree is successful, its success is dependent on one subself shutting out another subself entirely, which can lead to frustration, depression, low self-worth, and a vague feeling of incompleteness. A part of the person is in prison and deprived of its rights.

But will power decrees don't usually work, because in most cases the commands can be carried out only while the top dog is able to mobilize more energy than the bottom dog. So the bottom dog, having no platform for negotiation, lies in wait for the moment when the top dog weakens, and then strikes.

It is pure sabotage. Subjugated subselves find an occasion to break through when the dominant subself is tired, weak, distracted, or too socially embarrassed to interfere. Then the hostage grabs the gun: Dieters suddenly gorge themselves, smokers smoke, and drinkers drink. Work-avoiding subselves find fascinating diversions to avoid the required task, or they simply throw an exhaustion fit and immobilize the whole person. The point is that will power constitutes an undemocratic, unstable wrenching of your mechanism for choice from the committee of subselves, an unfriendly takeover.

You can make or break habits through will power alone, but you shouldn't. In will power resolutions, we direct our will power energy at one subself and (once again) leave that subself out of establishing our goals and schedules.

My students engage in growth projects, many of which involve establishing a new habit or breaking an old one. Many prefer to start by using raw will power. They simply recognize a need, set up a plan, and follow it. Sometimes it works—when both subselves recognize how much better they feel losing weight, or exercising, or not smoking, the psycho-physical reinforcement dissolves the opposition. But in the majority of cases, the will power project flounders and dies because reinforcement is slow in coming, and the habit-making/breaking subself fills this gap by maintaining a high level of personal energy to overcome the resister subself.

After a day, a week, or a month, the constant will power energy fades, and the resister subself comes forward and has its way, as it has done in the past. It knows the routine. It was not included, consulted, or recognized as legitimate in the original commitment, and as the project progressed and the old hungers grew stronger, they were squelched by the will-power-wielding subself. The resister feels no obligation or sense of participation in making the project work, and eventually accepts its given role— that of an opponent—and blocks the action. However, when all involved subselves agree to create a new habit or break an old one, the result is unopposed unity.

We are always so proud of our will power, but it is pure self-subjugation, and even when it works, the drain on energy and harmony are seldom worth the price.

Set sensible, shared goals, not monolithic ideals that become edicts. Create them first in the subself chairs, where harmony and health are equal partners.

CHAPTER EIGHT

Subself Occasions: When to Use the Chairs

Today my boyfriend was getting on my last nerve. I didn't want to lose control, so I went into his bathroom and. . . after going over a subself session quietly by myself, I went to him and told him I had a problem that I would like to discuss and wanted to know when he had time to discuss it. It worked—and I didn't fly off the handle! I was so happy because that means I'm making progress.

—Student log

We have dealt with three of the many occasions in which subself negotiation leads to integration and harmony. We started with the blocked-action negotiations because they are probably the most common subself occasions—conflicts involving choices.

But there is a wide variety of subself conflicts and we get our clues to them through our guilt, embarrassment, remorse, regret, vacillation, self-anger, avoidance, paralysis, and irritability. Below are some key phrases that indicate our subself separation:

Why can't I seem to . . . ?

I should . . . but I don't want to.

What's bothering me?

Which way do I go?

I've got mixed feelings about that.

Now what made me do that?

Let's look at the remaining assortment of subself occasions.

EQUAL-VALENCE DECISIONS

An equal-valence decision is not a conflict, it is a dilemma. You have come down to two (or more) options, and you can't for the life of you decide which is the better choice. Do you buy the Chevrolet or the Ford? Do you choose the small college or the large one? Do you spend your vacation in Hawaii or Machu Picchu? Do you go to your city or your country relatives for Thanksgiving dinner?

When you feel confused and paralyzed by choices like these, go to the chairs and put one of your options in each chair. You will be surprised at how fast you will realize which subselves are backing which choice. It is often as important to discover who's supporting which side as it is to solve the problem. This new self-knowledge clears away the muddy ambiguity of what seemed at first to be equal-valence decisions.

SELF-CRITICISM

Here is a subself discussion with a new element. Self-criticism usually concerns the *past,* not the present or future. You have done or continuously do something that bothers you enough that you think you should examine it. In fact, you may already have one subself exploding with remorse or feeling guilty about something another subself has been doing.

69

Getting over the guilt

When you do not deal openly with them, these feelings of criticism, remorse, and guilt can pollute your sense of self-worth. If you do not separate the subselves into who is responsible for a controversial action or attitude and who is feeling critical, you are stuck with a spiraling plunge of spirit. You tell yourself, "I shouldn't have done that"; "I was stupid"; "I'm terrible"; "I can't forgive myself for being so insensitive."

When entering the subself chairs with self-criticism, you start by knowing that *some* subself must have chosen to perform the act in question, so one chair goes to *"I am the one who did it,"* and the other chair goes to *"I don't do this sort of thing,"* or *"Did do"* and *"Wouldn't have done."* (Be sure to get these names written on the chairs—in the regrets and defenses that follow, you could get lost in chair contamination.)

If you did do something that you now feel guilty about, you must have had some good personal reasons or strong feelings for doing it. Find the voice in you that says "It seemed the right thing to do at the time." Give this voice a chair, a subself. Don't overwhelm it with waves of shame from the outraged subself.

Objective self-evaluation

Self-criticism doesn't always have to be linked with guilt. It may simply involve your objectively reviewing a performance you gave or a project you have completed. Using two chairs helps you to separate the different standards that you use in judging your best efforts. Even while writing this manual, I used dialogues when I stopped for a coffee break:

YOU MUST USE THE CHAIRS

Editor me: Aren't we getting a little wordy and pompous in that last section?

Writer me: Well, maybe so, but I have to let it flow as it comes. You'll get your chance to chop it later.

Editor me: It would save me a lot of work if you'd write a wee bit crisper.

Writer me: OK, but I don't want subself theory to sound like a glib game.

Editor me: Yeah, but you want people to read it, don't you? Lighten up!

The point is that you are questioning rather than criticizing yourself. Part of you is likely to support anything you do, and another part will feel free to question. This kind of separation tends to put your creativity into high gear rather than throwing you into self-doubt and misgivings.

HAPPY TALK

It is true that your subselves readily speak out when there is a conflict and seem to fade into each other during times of harmony. However, don't restrict your subself conversations to crisis situations. It is good preparation for the moments of confrontation to keep up a daily dialogue among the subselves, emphasizing agreement as well as disagreement: happy talk.

Here are some easy ways to promote happy talk between the subselves.

Self-admiration

If you have no issue-specific subselves at hand, go into a Parent/Child dialogue in which each subself says quite honestly to the other what it likes about the other.

> *Parent:* I like it when you tell me I'm being pompous. I have a hard time seeing it myself.

> *Child:* I like it when you let me say outrageous things at meetings without apologizing for me.

Self-congratulation

We seldom accomplish great things with one subself dragging the others behind it. Great accomplishments take all of the cooperative efforts of the subselves. When you are feeling a sense of achievement, open up a dialogue between the subselves in which they can express their appreciation of their good work.

> *A:* It's only 10:00 A.M. and we've gotten in two good hours of writing.

> *B:* Well, I love working in the valley away from all the distractions at home.

> *A:* We could finish another section by noon.

> *B:* Right, but I'm a little groggy. Let's have coffee first.

YOU MUST USE THE CHAIRS

Thank-you notes

Appreciation for sacrifices made is a good occasion for happy talk. One subself can be glad that the other persuaded it to:

- take a few days off
- finish a hard job
- terminate a relationship
- sacrifice a weekend to help a friend move
- avoid a risky business deal

ANXIETY AND UNLOCATED STRESS

Finally, we have an important role for you-the-Adult in subself negotiation. Your Adult subself can help when there's no conflict and no dilemma, but the presence of anxiety or some unlocated stress tells you that you have a problem you can't zero in on. These are the days in your life when you can hear yourself saying, "There's something wrong. What is it? I'm feeling down (or tense). Why? I can't put my finger on it."

In this situation you put your anxiety in one chair and your Adult in the other. The Adult acts like a therapist to the anxious or stressed subself. As therapist, the Adult probes, asks questions, and recognizes the feelings of the anxious subself. It tries to lead that subself into defining the problem, uncovering its causes, exploring alternative solutions, and choosing a way to relieve the situation. The physical presence of your

Adult can add structure to your thinking, keeping you from winding up in those tight little circles of thought that go nowhere.

This is an excellent role for the Adult. It is concerned and caring and has the most unbiased view of external conditions, but is not the one holding the bad feelings. If you can imagine yourself helping someone else in peer therapy, then you can use those same skills on a needy subself within you. Use everything you know about how people go about helping other people, but do it in the chairs, not in your head.

So far we have been using the P-A-C subselves as our supporting models in subself negotiation. But several other subself theories hold that there is one subself within each of us who carries our deepest wisdom and that this wisdom is considerable in all of us. In psychosynthesis, the therapist asks the client to assume the role of the "wise old man or woman" within and answer deep questions from this subself. On occasion in gestalt therapy, the therapist will get up from his or her own chair and say to the client, "Here, sit in my chair and tell yourself what you should do next."

The Adult in you has an additional advantage over an outside therapist. Your Adult lives in your own head with you, and whatever subself is speaking will find it hard to play evasive games with the Adult. The Adult will not tolerate games and will make comments like, "Come on, now, don't con me with that martyr talk. You know better than that and so do I."

Keep in mind the banner statement of psychologist Carl Rogers in his widely used nondirective therapy: "He who has the problem has the solution." The therapist's main job is to tap that wisdom, not supply it. Who would know better where to look than your own wisest subself?

YOU MUST USE THE CHAIRS

Oh God! I think I finally realized what is up! I had to sit right down and write it. While doing my subself negotiation something came out. I guess I knew it all along, but just didn't want to admit it. Anyway, my GIVE IT UP self was arguing with my GUITAR PLAYING self, and my GUITAR PLAYING self said, "But Phil wants you to do it." And that's when I realized that I wasn't playing for myself, but I was playing for my boyfriend. He was the one I think that really wanted me to play. I mean, I love playing, but I am doing it more for him than I am for me, and I won't get anywhere with that. Now I've started doing it for myself, but to be honest I'm a singer and that's what I really enjoy doing. So I will play guitar but on a part-time basis.

—Student log

BURNOUT

The *player* can complain about *worker* burnout ("You're working us to death!"), and the worker can complain about player burnout ("I can't stand working all day and having you drag us out to parties all night"), but the most common cause of burnout is hard work. And yet, hard work alone does not burn people out when all of the subselves are cooperating harmoniously. People can work murderously hard all their lives and thrive on it so long as the forward energy is not slowed down by drag or resistance. We can tap into enormous energy reserves when there is no drag. When all of our energy is going in the same direction, there is flow, not friction. Time dissolves, food becomes an incidental, and sleep becomes an

75

interruption. We have found a unity of mind, body, and process.

What causes burnout is energy being placed *against* energy, with subselves competing furiously for our vitality and creating star bursts of work and play, flashy but life consuming. Our inner dilemma is resistance, friction, heat, and, finally, burnout.

In the case of a worker and player competing for energy, neither is likely to call a halt for fear of having to compromise its own ends. Your Adult, or wiser subself, may have to step forward and say, "You two are destroying us all in this cattle vs. sheep energy war, and you've got to do something about it. I invite you both to the chairs and leave you to it."

SPEAKING THE ANGER

Anger is not an emotion that is socially acceptable except in short, well-founded bursts. We are more frequently angry internally than externally. We become angry at things, people, situations, and ourselves. When anger smolders inside us without our expressing it, it can grow from a distracting nuisance to a major warping of our personality. Subself negotiation is a safe ground for expressing our anger, questioning it, processing it, and dissolving it.

One especially useful process is discovering *attack* thoughts and processing them in the chairs. Many people discover their attack thoughts while driving their car—they fume at other drivers. I catch myself in anger while walking the dog. I gradually realize that I am indulging in a diabolical fantasy about what I would like to do to parked cars that block my passage on the public sidewalk. Suddenly another voice speaks up: "Whoa! Where's all this fury coming from? Why are you so incensed? We're getting our adrenaline up over a foolish anger."

I know then that it is time to talk it out.

Perhaps you are feeling ill-treated by a love partner or a coworker. Although you have chosen to react calmly and rationally externally, you can feel a subself fuming, not only at the situation but at the subself who chooses to be passive and agreeable in the face of injustice. Surprising revelations often emerge from taking the subself chairs at this point, with *mad me* in one chair and *be reasonable me* in the other.

Thoroughly processing an immediate anger also can uncover deeper frustrations and resentments, feelings that you can and should deal with for the sake of your inner harmony and outer sanity.

LONG- AND SHORT-TERM PLANNING

Complicated schemes and plans often get lost in our consciousness and memory. Details are clearer and more easily recalled when we talk them out. But who among our friends wants to listen to our plan for a busy evening—or a ten-year program? The participants themselves, our own subselves, are our most eager and helpful allies.

DEPRESSION AND GRIEF

Love, anger, depression, fear, trauma, shock, and grief—all are powerful yet highly private emotions. They need processing without censorship. There is no one we can talk to as openly as our own subselves.

- Let the *grieving* subself speak to the *life must go on* subself.

- Let the *depressed* subself unload on the *optimistic* subself.

- Let the *rejection-fearing* subself speak frankly to the *lonely and needing* subself.

COMMITMENT

One of our most common subself splits is between the part of us who wants to be committed in love to another person and the subself who wants to be free. Often we impulsively commit to or reject other people, depending on which subself is in control at the moment. We approach our friends, lovers, family, and partners in life from a much more solid and reliable base when we have first done our homework about commitment in the unhurried privacy of subself negotiation.

ILL HEALTH

We are familiar with psychosomatic illnesses and the power of the mind to heal physical injuries, diseases, and disabilities. Our immune system is known to be as sensitive psychologically as it is physically. Ill health takes as much mental processing as it does physical and chemical therapy. Biofeedback training has been highly effective in controlling bodily functions.

Subself negotiation is pure, uncut dialogue among the inner forces that have psychological control over the body. It should be part of any healing therapy.

YOU MUST USE THE CHAIRS

Speak to your body—your heart, your tennis elbow, your blood, your fatigue, your acid stomach. If you get no answer, try a different approach. Look for a *causal* self and a *healing* self.

- I am *healthy* me.
  I want to speak to *ailing* me.

- I am *helpless* me.
  I want to speak to *disease-resistant* me.

- I am *frightened* me.
  I want to speak to *me-in-pain.*

Give your healing energy a specific focus—a laser beam of personal inquiry. Try to awaken and draw up to a conscious level the parts of the mind that directly control, adjust, or command the body.

PROCESSING EXTERNAL CRITICISM

The two-chair method is also a popular and effective catalyst to interpersonal confrontation. You can use what I call the fair- fight technique in resolving differences between yourself and husbands and wives, parents and children, bosses and employees, and other intimates. (See *Let's Have It Out: The Bare-Bones Manual of Fair Fighting,* by this author.)

But many participants in person-to-person confrontation are not prepared internally to discuss difficult issues with another person because they have not worked out in private their own priorities, inner choices, and limits of compromise. Subself negotiation should precede person-to-person confrontation and also should follow a fair fight so you can process your personal reactions to the confrontation.

YOU MUST USE THE CHAIRS

By first discussing issues among the subselves, each partner in a fair fight comes to the chairs from a more solid, stable, and centered base. We should know exactly what we want before we ask for it. We also should know what we are prepared to offer on our side of a compromise in any important relationship. Use both chairs yourself before you offer one of them to a partner.

WHO AM I REALLY? THE SEARCH FOR MEANING

There are deeper issues of existence and meaning working in all of us than whether we will work or play this weekend or which resort will get our holiday business. We house in our subselves all of our personal values about the deepest philosophical questions of humanity: selfishness and commitment to others, being and doing, the balance of yin and yang, the varieties and degrees of morality, honesty, risk, and pleasure.

Each of us is his or her own best source of the true nature of these discussions because each of us has only one experience with humanity—the thoughts, feelings, and actions of our inner selves.

Do we each know where we stand as a total person when the doorbell rings and we find waiting for us a missionary, an environmentalist, a civil-rights activist, a party worker, a petitioner, an irate neighbor, or a person with a gun?

Subself negotiation and integration can be a lifetime of taking the chairs—one issue at a time. For starters, we might bring to the chairs some of our outstanding paradoxes, such as:

- the *masculine* me and the *feminine* me
- the *selfish* me and the *giving* me
- the *passive* me and the *active* me

80

- the *cooperative* me and the *competitive* me
- the *intuitive* me and the *rational* me
- the *believing* me and the *skeptical* me

We are each so multifaceted and complex that we often are disposed to let the dominant energy force of the moment dictate our daily courses of action. But true integration and self-harmony are tied to self-knowing and self-understanding.

81

CHAPTER NINE

Variations on Subself Negotiation

In subself negotiation there are several possible elaborations and substitutions, but they are for special purposes. The simple two-chair technique should be the starting point for every person who is searching for subself separation and resolution.

IN YOUR HEAD

Yes, you can do subself negotiation in your head while driving your car or walking down the street, but the temptation is to try this too soon. First you should be adept at working in the chairs, and my estimate is that this takes about six months to a year. Then, almost automatically, you will find identifiable subselves coming forward for short, clear exchanges when you are alone and thinking of problems.

AUDIOTAPE AND VIDEOTAPE

Speaking to yourself on audiotape and videotape has both advantages and disadvantages. The usefulness of taping lies in

YOU MUST USE THE CHAIRS

your being able to replay the negotiations and pick out strengths and weaknesses in your arguments. One dramatic effect of taping is that you actually see and hear the differences in subself personalities, and you begin to appreciate the intensity of the feelings coming through: the whining or petulant subself, the nagging and scolding subself, and so on.

But the disadvantages are that you might lose some spontaneity both in the exercise of setting up your machinery and in the temptation to role-play and perform for the camera and microphone. In addition, not everything that your subselves wish to say may be fit to print, and there is the danger that you might censor your subself discussion because it is going on tape.

Videotape playback is a good method of observing vital but subtle body language, which reveals subself signals. Dr. Fritz Perls, in his gestalt therapy sessions, used visual cues given by the subselves to aid in the therapy. He believed that when a subject was not being totally honest, he or she would signal this in some way, usually in body language. A subself pretending to be open and receptive but whose legs were crossed, arms folded, and upper body twisted away from the confrontation was signaling that no matter how open its comments, it was feeling closed and protective.

Perls also believed that subself splits followed body planes; that is, at any given moment, one subself might be controlling the upper body and another the lower body. One subself might be controlling the entire left side of the body and the other the right side. When he found these visual splits, such as a client sitting on her hands or another dragging his feet or another squeezing one hand with the other, he would ask the client to let these body parts speak:

YOU MUST USE THE CHAIRS

Therapist: Be your left hand, and speak to your right hand.

Left hand subself: You're squeezing me too tight; you're hurting me.

Therapist: Now switch chairs. Be your right hand and answer.

Right hand subself: I need to control you. I'm trying to remind you that you are about to say something neither of us wants to hear. I didn't mean to hurt you.

In watching yourself on videotape, you might pick up on some of these visual body clues and become more sensitive to your subselves signaling conflicts through body language.

Dr. Stewart Shapiro, who has developed a style of subself negotiation, recommends a variation called "mirror talk," in which you stand squarely in front of a mirror and address the image therein. He recommends it for exercises involving the total self. First you tell the mirror image the positive things you feel about yourself. Then you answer, still watching the mirror, with your negative comments about yourself. In this way, you get a very real visual picture of who is speaking and reacting. It's hard not to be authentic when you are looking directly at yourself.[1]

THE THIRD CHAIR

The problem with using a third chair is that it tends to sap vital energy from direct confrontation. Rather than being an aid, the third chair often becomes a detour or escape valve. We

---

1. Stewart Shapiro, *The Selves Within You* (Explorations Institute, 1976).

know that we have more than two subselves. Eric Berne identifies as many as thirteen. There are occasions for three-way
discussions among three separate selves, but effective subself
confrontation is a taxing exercise—it takes intense concentration to keep the subselves wholly separated and to remember
what each of them has said. Adding a third chair raises the
complexity significantly, and should be reserved for special
needs and used only by accomplished two-chair negotiators.

One way to use the third chair without having it interfere
with the process is to leave the third chair empty, but in place,
until the two speaking subselves have finished. Then get up
and sit in the third chair and speak to the other two subselves
as an observer who had sat through the entire session. You
might choose one of the following roles to get into this: the
outside observer, the *wise old man* or *woman,* the *chairper-
son,* the *overseer,* the *Adult.*

USING A HELPER

Obviously, if you have a therapist or trained subself nego-
tiator available, he or she can be enormously useful sitting in
the third chair. But the joy of two-chair work is that it belongs
entirely to you. You are not led or guided.

Working alone, you will get into stalemates and occasional
confusion. This is how it should be—the subselves must train
themselves to get out of these predicaments without depending on a guide. And once again, when you have an audience,
there is a temptation to perform and please, which leads to
artificial and contrived solutions that do not hold up after you
leave the chairs.

But there is one excellent advantage to having a helper. He
or she can operate like a traffic cop or an umpire between the

subselves, calling errors of contamination. ("Wait a moment, who just said that, *Student you* or *Fun-loving you*? Are you in the right chair for what you just said?") The helper should not make contributions to the argument or suggestions on how to proceed, except when trying to keep the subself separation clean. He or she may interrupt with a suggestion to switch chairs when (1) a question has been asked, (2) there is a long thinking pause, or (3) one subself begins giving the other's arguments.

The helper must let the subselves struggle and find their way. Any substantive external suggestions will distract you from important inner processes.

WRITING TO YOURSELF

Some of us feel more comfortable writing to ourselves than talking. It is a more leisurely, slow-paced, and orderly style, and some people do it well. You may sit down once a day and construct a subself dialogue in the style of a daily log or diary. This has the advantage of being a regular and systematic process. Writing down your argument also tends to serve your rational subself well because the rational subself is slanted toward lists and logic. But what the diary misses is the intensity of feeling that is available in an oral conversation. Writing is one-dimensional compared to your full involvement when speaking from the subself chairs.

Set up the log like a play script, with each character labeled before it speaks. Some people can get the intensity of feeling into a written dialogue, but often this evolves into being overdramatic and overwritten, so that the final script sounds more like a melodrama than an honest dialogue. The trick is to write as genuinely and spontaneously as you speak. One student of mine who prefers writing to talking out a dialogue switches back and forth between a black- and a red-ink pen to indicate change of voice.

Another way to approach subself writing is to let your Adult do the writing, as if observing a Parent-Child dialogue, like this:

My responsible self is saying that . . .

My needing self is saying that . . .

YOU MUST USE THE CHAIRS

CHAPTER TEN

Going beyond Conscious Subselves

Y ou can use the subself chairs for three practical techniques that do not directly involve the conscious subselves in one or both chairs. These techniques, *dream work, fantasy conversations,* and *rehearsals,* all begin with role-playing, and yet in the course of each of them, real subselves may take over the roles and participate.

DREAM INTERPRETATION

One important theory in dream interpretation says that when you dream, you are talking to yourself in a coded drama that disguises the subselves trying to communicate with you. Every part of most of your dreams is actually a part of yourself. If you dream of your mother, this theory maintains that there is a part of you who wishes to act out some thought or feeling, and that part of you takes the form of your mother.

Should you dream that you are walking down a gravel road under some oak trees, carrying a heavy suitcase, you would use the chairs to actually take the part of *You walking,* You *the gravel road,* You *the oak trees,* and You *the suitcase.* Each speaks separately.

PULLING YOURSELF TOGETHER

Me walking: I don't know why I'm walking down this road, but I seem to be determined to get somewhere up ahead.

Me the gravel road: I am not the easiest thing to walk on, but I give you a direction, and if you can stand the inconvenience of my sharp stones, I'll get you where you want to go.

Me the oak tree: I can protect you from the sun and the rain. I'm very, very old, put here years ago to be beautiful and useful.

Me the suitcase: I'm worn and battered, but my hardware is strong, and I'm used to carrying the load for you.

Me the heaviness in the suitcase: You can't see me, but I'm nothing but a load of useless bricks. If you knew how unnecessary I am, you'd spill me out on the road and travel much lighter.

After taking inventory of the dream elements, you can enter into a dialogue between two of the parts, such as *Me walking* discussing why it is carrying a heavy load with *Me the bricks.*

The final step is to ask yourself, "What part of me is a heavy load that I must carry unnecessarily, and what part of me is willing to carry this load without even knowing what it is?"

The more recent the dream, the better, and there appears to be special value in placing recurring dreams in the chairs, but not old dreams that you have stopped dreaming.

If you intend to interpret your dreams, you should make this intention known to yourself every night before retiring and then keep a notebook and pencil by the bed. When you

YOU MUST USE THE CHAIRS

wake up from a dream, write it down immediately so that you can interpret it the next day.

Begin every dream interpretation session by retelling the complete dream to yourself, aloud, using present-tense verbs ("I am walking down this gravel road, and it seems so long, and I can't see the end of it," and so on). Then use the subself chairs to separate the dream into its parts and conduct a dialogue.

The payoff, of course, is asking, "What part of me is saying this?" This is the point when subselves may come forward to reveal their roles in the dream.

FANTASY CONVERSATIONS

Fantasy conversations involve role-playing as well as your subself skills. Place your total self in one chair and imagine that a real person whom you need to talk to, but can't, is in the other chair. One of the most effective uses of this method is for speaking to a now-dead parent with whom you have important unfinished business. ("Mother, I need to tell you how much I love you. I never had the courage to when you were alive," or "Father, you never knew how much I resented you when you left us. Now I want to tell you.")

Then you move to the other chair and answer yourself from what you believe your parent would say. This can become a highly moving, cathartic, and healing negotiation.

You can try the same exercise with a lost or departed intimate, one who has rejected you or whom you have rejected, a divorced spouse, or any other unattainable person, even the hit- and-run driver who ran over your dog.

90

CONFLICT REHEARSAL

Using two chairs for subself negotiation is closely related to fair-chair fighting, in which real partners take the chairs to discuss problem areas between them. Rehearsing a fair-chair confrontation alone, before you confront a real partner, is useful in that it sharpens your arguments, improves your self-control, bolsters your confidence, and tests your subself support for the conflict. When you sit in your opponent's chair and answer yourself, you begin to see new dimensions to the issue. You begin to understand your opponent's point of view, needs, and problem of confronting you.

A full rehearsal of an upcoming confrontation begins with your sitting in your own chair and starting with "I'm having a problem with something you are doing and need to talk about it with you." From there on you proceed as you intend to when the real confrontation arises. (See *Let's Have It Out* for good outlines in constructive confrontation.)

To get the most out of this conflict rehearsal, you should conduct it twice: first, the worst scenario, and second, the best scenario. Suppose you are determined to confront your boss or superior at work. You perceive him or her as intimidating and stubborn. Play it first that way, as a worst scenario. Then play it again as you would *hope* your boss might be, realistically but also optimistically.

There is still another surprise to this technique: People who use it often change their whole approach to the upcoming confrontation, or, having gotten the whole thing off their chest, they discover ways to solve their problem without having to confront at all.

91

CHAPTER ELEVEN

Re-Union

You've read the book, and now I can say some things you might not have found credible before. For one thing, I hope that by this time you have sat down in two chairs and talked with yourself.

The first thing you may have discovered is that two-chair subself negotiation is real, not a gimmick or a game, and that the subselves who speak are complete personalities with legitimate biases. Subself negotiation is primarily a discovery or recognition of the plurality within each of us.

- It is a process of understanding and appreciating the fullness and complexity that you may only have known as swarming fragments of self.

Overheard subself: "You really are there, aren't you, not just a voice."

- It is a process of creating new relationships and new solutions that you not only can live with but also can thrive on.

Overheard subself: "I feel such new energy just talking to you."

- It is a process of reasoning; subself negotiation clarifies thought, gives it order, sequence, and completion.

Overheard subself: "That's something I hadn't considered. Let's put that on the list."

- It is a process of revealing, uncovering, and calling out the forces within you that often are reluctant to be recognized.

Overhead subself: "I never knew until now that you felt so strongly about this."

- It is a process of friendship, caring, and tenderness. The subselves are you, and they are the brothers and sisters that make up the whole you. When you allow them to settle their differences peacefully and fairly, they show and speak their loving need for one another.

Overheard subself: "My God, I feel as if I've just found a real friend!"

- It is a democratizing process in which a recognition of rights, legitimacy, equality, and internal justice replaces crippling power struggles.

Overheard subself: "Sure, it's OK with me, now that I'm part of the process of deciding."

93

Subself negotiation is the re-union of the self. *Re*-union because union was our first consciousness; later, the necessities and complexities of life gave us differing goals and purposes, causing genuine divisions—unattended splits—within us. For re-union to occur, we must raise those divisions to conscious physical entities, the subselves, so they can find their way back together again.

The controversies about the self are endless. Is there really a self? If so, where is it found within us? Despite these unknowns, we know that each of us is and has an identity, that our total consciousness revolves around this identity, and that it makes the choices that move us through our lives. It is this identity in each of us that struggles for survival, pleasure, meaning, and union.

It is time we introduced ourselves.

Today I started doing the subself talking in the book. You know, it's funny but it works! Really! When I sat down with myself, and let the part or subself who doesn't get to be heard a lot heard, it was such a freeing experience! Just to be able to say, "Pat, I need more control" was nice . . . . It worked, too. For a moment, I felt I had control over all of me.

—Student log

94

About the Author

Dr. Arthur S. Hough, Jr., is professor of communication at San Francisco State University and also has taught in this field at six other American universities. After having completed a B.S. in English Education at Rutgers University, he earned an M.A. and a Ph.D. in Communication Theory from Northwestern University and the University of Denver. He has received one national and three university awards for meritorious teaching.

Dr. Hough was a communication workshop leader at Esalen Institute and other growth centers in the 1960s and has since taught communication and counseling workshops for a dozen government agencies and independent organizations.

Among his publications are three other communication texts:

The Forgotten Choice: Breaking Through Paradigm to Human Potential

Let's Have It Out: The Bare-Bones Manual of Fair Fighting

Dynamic Silence: A First Book in Concentrative Meditation